How to Generate
Passive Income

Quit Your Job and Start Your Online Empire

Table of Contents

Introduction

Chapter One: Making Money from a YouTube Channel

Understanding Your Audience

Six Ways to Make Money

How to Not Sell Out

Chapter Two: Make Online Courses

Choose a Topic

Market Research

Outline

Delivery

Creation

Sale

Upload

Few Final Steps

Chapter Three: Selling a Product You Invent

Research

Presentation

Other Tips

Chapter Four: Write a Book

Research

Create

Publish

Launch and Market

Other Tips

Chapter Five: Make a Blog

Advertisements

Affiliate Program

Sell Digital Products

Sell Memberships

Blogging for Credibility

Other Tips

Chapter Six: Sell Photos and Videos

Microstock Sites

Selling Videos

Chapter Seven: Sell Online Coaching

Build an Audience

Launch Premium Offer

Update Your Pages

Post on Social Media Outlets

Ads

Launch

Chapter Eight: Dropshipping Store

Pick the Right Product

Create a Professional Website

Find the Right Supplier

Be Consistent

Conclusion

Introduction

If you would like to make more money with less fuss, then keep reading...

In today's world, making ends meet is very difficult for some people. You work eight hours a day or more with little time to yourself. At the end of the month, you are left with very little cash to save for a rainy day, let alone your holiday. However, there are people out there who seem to do nothing and yet money flows into their pockets endlessly. What is going on here?

Can you imagine spending your day sunbathing at a distant tropical location while still making thousands above and apart from your average wage? It is possible and does not have to be a distant dream because the solution is this: passive income.

Passive income is earnings derived from businesses that you are not actively involved in. That means you can make a sizeable profit while spending little to no time actively engaged in the business. That also means you can easily expand your passive income channel and make even more money!

It is time to put down that buzzing phone for a bit and start planning alternative ways you can make a living without spending 8 hours a day doing something you don't even enjoy doing. It is time to get your head into the game and find out how you can dramatically increase your income. In fact, perhaps you can even monetise your hobby. It is time to start thinking about passive income.

In this book, you will discover:

- How to generate ads revenue from YouTube videos

- How to join an affiliate program and make money from your blogs

- How to get paid teaching or coaching others online

- How you can sell your creative writing on Amazon

And so much more!

Just picture it now, curled up with a loved one, and sunbathing at a distant tropical location, without a worry in your mind while your phone only buzzed to tell you that you have made another sale. Get started today on generating passive income. You deserve a break from the hectic life at the office.

So, if you're ready to increase the amount of money you make dramatically with little to no efforts, read on!

Chapter One: Making Money from a YouTube Channel

On a social media whose 1.3 billion users consume over five billion videos daily averaging at 40 minutes of view time per user, there is a lot of potential to start making passive income using YouTube. Of course, you will not be making tens of millions yearly like some of the top YouTubers unless you pour the majority of your time into it. You can still make a comfortable amount off of the website. Before you do, make sure you understand your audience demographics and try to cater to their interests.

Understanding Your Audience

Your audience and your channel are interrelated. As you grow your channel that is catered toward a specific niche, more viewers who are interested in this field will eventually flock to your channel. This also means that it can be difficult if you want to branch out to other areas. As you grow, you need to pay close attention to gender, age, geographic location, and watch time. All of these factors will give you an idea of what kind of videos would be most effective for your audience.

Six Ways to Make Money

With a good audience base, you can really start to generate a steady revenue flow. There are six ways to do so:

- Ads revenue: Set yourself up as a YouTube Partner via the Creator Studio. Create an AdSense account and opt into Google's advertising network. Then, a green "$" should appear next to your video in the Video Manager.

- Selling products or merchandise: Generates both income and exposure; all you need is a solid audience base that is willing to support you by buying your merchandise.

- Crowdfund your projects: You can ask your audience or others to help fund your projects through crowdfunding sites such as Kickstarter, or Indiegogo.

- Fan funding: Similarly, you can create a channel in which your fans can donate to you. If the content is good, your fans are more likely to donate. Patreon is a great place to start.

- Licensing: If you create a viral video, you can license it to media outlets for money. Junken Media is a good place to host your videos for easier access to potential buyers.

- Influencer or affiliate program: Partner with brands, which also caters to your audience. Influencer marketplace includes Grapevine Logic, Famebit, Channel Pages, and Crowdtap.

How to Not Sell Out

Your audience makes or breaks your channel, so no matter how hard you try to make money, never make it obvious to your audience that you care more about making money than entertainment. All of the above methods of monetising require you to maintain your balance between content integrity and the fact that you are monetising. There are several approaches you can take to accomplish this.

- Call to action: Be subtle and suggest what your audience should do (click the like button, subscribe, etc.)

- YouTube cards: Set them to pop up at the right moment with relevant content without distracting the audience.

- Links: Add links to your other sources of YouTube income (Patreon, online shop, etc.)

- Go beyond YouTube: Grow social media following outside of YouTube for more awareness.

Chapter Two: Make Online Courses

There are certain things that textbooks cannot teach a person. This is where you come in to provide practical knowledge in any particular field. In reality, everyone has something new to learn. With so many competitors though, you need to make your own courses stand out from others.

Choose a Topic

Prepare a list of all the things you know. It does not have to be academic (economy, law, etc.). You can teach others about your hobbies, such as golf or painting.

Market Research

Do your research and see if the course you are selling will fly. Many people will be curious about your field, but few will be willing to pay to know more about it. Before you start sinking your time into it, make sure that your audience is willing to spend money.

Outline

Next, think of what to put in your courses. The content should cover all the important aspects of the topic and be in-depth, much different from your casual blog posts.

You may also need to organise your courses into modules and lessons. A module is a subtopic, and the lessons under said module should provide all the details of that subtopic. For example, if you plan to have a course on creative writing, then your lessons would include "How to Use Emotive Languages".

Delivery

Online courses are more flexible because you have access to text, video, audio, infographics, checklists, or other media. It is up to you to figure out which format or approach is best for the course. In some cases, there is more than one method that works best for the lesson. Text and video are commonly used.

Creation

Being creative is what you will likely sink most of your time into because you need to create the bulk of your content. To look professional, stick to a particular colour theme that suits the topic as well as adding a logo that appears in all lessons. Make sure to proofread your lessons, watch your videos, and generally review all your materials to weed out errors.

Sale

There are many ways you can start to sell your lessons. You can create your website (Wordpress, Squarespace, Wix, etc.) and sell your services from there. You can use an online course service (Udemy, Skillshare, etc.) Another method is to use sites such as Teachable or Ruzuku, which combine the control of your own site with the ease of use and speed of Skillshare. Whatever you do, make sure you read their terms of service.

Upload

With a platform to host your lessons, the next step is to upload them. If you can customise your courses, such as adding a colour scheme or logo, then you should because it helps you create your own brand.

Few Final Steps

In the end, you just need to get the word out, which involves creating a plan on how you can reach those who may be interested in paying for your course. It also pays to keep your course updated, so check your content every few months or so.

Chapter Three: Selling a Product You Invent

Sometimes, you have an idea for a product that has never been on the market before. Making passive income from a product that you invent is similar to owning a dropshipping store, which we will discuss in Chapter Eight. To start making money from this channel, you need to do the following:

Research

First, find out as much as possible about the market or the industry and how your product comes in. Study the markets for your product and determine how or whether your products can be sold nationally or internationally, or only to a specific market. Introduce this idea to your family and friends and listen to their input.

Study your key competitors and what they sell. Determine the strengths and weaknesses of your products compared to those of your competitors. Try to look into the quality, features or ease of use of your product.

After that, study the legal side of things. Check if you can get a patent for your product or whether you may infringe the rights of existing patents. If everything is clear, you can proceed to obtain a "patent pending" for your product. This is basically a preliminary patent you can use to protect your idea at the pre-production stage. Also try to get a trademark if you need to protect certain words, phrase, or symbols associated with your product.

Presentation

Next, prepare a presentation about your product. It should be between two to five-page sales sheet with information about what materials are needed to produce your invention, the features, benefits, as well as the status of trademarks or patents. At this stage, make sure to have your prototype product ready for demonstration.

From there, look for manufacturers who produce and sell products in the same category as yours. Try to gather at least 30 manufacturers you can contact.

Evaluate their suitability based on size, location, reputation, etc. With this information, you can determine which one is most suited for the sale of your product.

Next, call some of the manufacturers and set up an appointment with them so you can present your products. Make sure that the marketing, sale, production or engineering executives are present at the meeting as they will determine if your product will fly or not.

If things go well, then one of the manufacturers will take you up on your offer. Then, it is just a matter of selling your product to them. You need to work out the details of the sale, such as payments or royalties. Make sure to have your attorney in the meeting to give you legal advice.

Other Tips

You can consider contacting intermediaries who specialise in connecting inventors to manufacturers. There are many of them out there, which can help you with the research process.

You can also consider manufacturing your own products. Sourcing the funding needed can be done on platforms such as Kickstarter, where you can demonstrate your products to the users there, and they decide if and how much they want to invest in your project. Of course, you still need to find a manufacturer to produce your products unless you can do it yourself somehow. If you decide to get the initial investment from Kickstarter, remember that you need to deliver the products to your backers.

Finally, beware of scammers in the invention industry, especially among the intermediaries we mentioned previously. However, quick research should allow you to determine if the company is legitimate.

Chapter Four: Write a Book

Making money from selling your books online can be a healthy source of income. The best thing about this is that anyone with a computer and an Internet connection can do it. Plus, there are many platforms out there where you can sell your work. Here is a quick 4-step guide to writing and selling your book.

Research

First, do your research. What kind of book do you want to sell? Fiction? Non-fiction? What topic do you wish to cover? Is it competitive? Who would like to buy your book? A good place to start researching and possible sell your book would be Amazon.

Create

This is the most time-consuming step of them all because you need to do proper research, plan your content, write, and then proofread your work. But if writing seems tedious, you can enlist the help of a ghostwriter. Ghostwriters specialise in writing content and you just need to pay a one-time fee. Plus, you will have all rights over the book transferred to you, meaning that the book is now yours and you can sell it under your name. All you need is to tell the ghostwriter the title of your book and perhaps notes on proposed content if you want it to cover specific topics.

Publish

After you have your book, it is time to upload it and start making money. If you upload your book on Amazon Kindle, then it is pretty straightforward. They have a platform called Kindle Direct Publishing (KDP), and you just need to register, submit tax information, upload your book and write a description for it. Other platforms should follow a similar process, so you should not have any trouble publishing your book elsewhere.

Launch and Market

The final step is to make sure that your book is discovered and bought consistently. It is worth taking your time to study how your book is listed so people can easily see it, and it varies between platforms. But Amazon or similar platforms are not the only way to promote your book. It is advisable to advertise on social media sites or your website.

Other Tips

Because the ebook market has many competitors, especially on Amazon, it is worth mentioning how you could get an edge over your competitors. Many authors are not good at marketing, so if you follow these four steps, your books should be a cut more convincing than others.

- Keywords: Just like Google, how readers discover your book depends on what they write in the search bar. If you know what your readers in your genre write in the search bar, make sure to include those words in the description of your book.

- Emotive language: Make sure that when your readers feel something when they read the description of your book. Strive to make them have questions and feel that the answers are given inside your book. A good way to do this is by using the first few sentences to paint a captivating image inside the head of your readers.

- Accolades: If you or your books have won any significant title such as bestseller, then make sure you mention it in the book description (preferably in the first sentence). In fact, anything is worth mentioning because you need to flaunt all of your achievements to convince your readers. Speaking of flaunting, if it is a nonfiction book, then consider adding biographical information to let the reader know more about the author.

- Comparable books: If you could write your description in a way that compares your work to that of the bestselling books in any genre, then there is a chance that your book may get recommended to the readers of those popular books.

Chapter Five: Make a Blog

Blogging is not as passive as people think. You still need to put in the work. You can make money from blogging in a similar way to YouTube.

Advertisements

The best way to start generating revenue from your site is through advertisements. You can either go for CPC, CPM, or private advertisements:

- CPC or PPC ads are cost per click or pay per click ads. Whenever a reader clicks on that advertisement, you get paid.

- CPM ads are advertisements that pay you whenever 1,000 readers view your ads.

- Private ads are the kinds of advertisements that you get from advertisers. With enough traffic, they may come to you and offer to sponsor you if you display their ads on your website.

Affiliate Program

Affiliate marketing is another way you can generate revenue from your blog. Similar to private advertisements, the process starts when an advertiser contacts you with an offer. They have a product or service to sell, and they need your help in getting the word out. You will get a commission for each sale if the buyer comes from your website. They know that because you will be given a unique link with your affiliate code. This code will be used to determine if the buyer comes from your site.

Sell Digital Products

If you have products to sell, then you should consider advertising it on your blog instead of having other advertisements clogging up space. In fact, your blog should be your base where you list all of your products or services from other chapters in this book. You can sell ebooks, online classes, coaching services, images, videos, music, apps, etc.

Whichever you choose to sell, just make sure that they are relevant to the content that you put out. Assume nothing and listen to your readers. Then strive to meet their demand.

Sell Memberships

Membership or subscription-based services that allow users access to a special section of your website. For example, if you run a career blog, then you can charge users a meagre amount every month so that they can access the job board that you host on your website. Of course, you need to make sure that your readers get more value from the membership than they can get for free elsewhere.

Blogging for Credibility

The best thing about blogging as a source of passive income is the fact that it can lead to many more opportunities for more sources of passive income. For example, if you run a fitness blog and you generate a hefty amount of traffic. At that point, you are considered a recognised figure in the fitness world.

When you have that level of authority, some people may approach you and offer you to co-author a book on related topics, or attend a conference as a guest speaker, etc.

While this is not how you should expect to make money from a blog, this is where most famous bloggers end up. You may be one of them if you put in the work. In fact, some of the most famous bloggers out there make between 4 to 7 figures just by selling their brands and content.

As mentioned previously, the only way to get there is by sticking your nose to the grindstone and work to build up your credibility. Many bloggers out there have created their sites and just let it sit there. You will need to sink in a huge amount of time while getting little to no pay.

Other Tips

If you seriously consider getting into blogging, there are a few more things you need to know:

Quality

No one is going to read badly-written content. The key is to please your audience because they are the ones who make you money, whether by clicking on ads or buying your products. The readers come first. Always.

Time

While you need to spend quite a bit of time on your blog, it is only a fraction of the success. It is all about managing and building relationships with your sponsors, affiliate partners, or other bloggers. So, make sure you balance your time properly.

Experiment

Sometimes, the best way to move forward is outside the comfort zone. What you read here may not work in your situation, so feel free to do what has worked for you so far. If you are at a loss, do something instead of nothing. At least you will know what you have done wrong and learn from your mistakes. Eventually, you will know what works for you and what does not.

Chapter Six: Sell Photos and Videos

Photographers often use social media or their own website to advertise their services by putting up their portfolio. You can take it a step further by selling images or videos directly from your websites in addition to your services. That way, your portfolio doubles as a gallery where people can browse and purchase any photos or videos that they like. There are a few ways you can sell photos online:

Microstock Sites

These sites used to be the only way you could sell photos or videos. You get to upload your work to their library and get paid based on sales. However, be extra careful when you read their policies. Most of the sites cut into your profit, up to 70%, and leaving you with a meagre 30% share.

In this day and age, sites such as Visual Society offer a more generous deal. You get to keep all of the revenue from your photo sales and you get to set your own rules and build a sizeable passive income stream with relative ease.

Selling Videos

Selling your videos requires more planning.

First, think of what you want to sell. What are you good at? Are you an entertainer or an educator? How good are you with programming, graphic design, or filmmaking? Are you a motivational speaker? After you have figured out what videos you want to make, test the water and see if your project will fly. To be exact, you need to look at other sites such as YouTube or Udemy to see if there is a demand for your kind of videos, and especially whether there are enough people who want to pay for it.

Plan Your Content

Next, you need to establish your course objective. Who is your target audience? What is the outcome for those who watch your videos? What special value will you have over your competition? When you have a clear idea of your content, it is time to think of the payment.

Decide on a Payment Structure

There are three ways to make money selling videos online: TVOD, AVOD, and SVOD. One-time purchase (TVOD) is a pay-per-view system. AVOD is an ad-based video on demand system, meaning that consumers do not pay to access it. SVOD is the most common because it is convenient for both the consumers and sellers. It is a subscription-based business.

Create Your Videos

When you have all the backend figured out, it is time to invest the time to make videos. If you are skilled, you can produce or edit your videos. Alternatively, you can get a video production team to handle it for you.

Final Few Steps

When you have polished your videos, you just need to upload them to the platform of your choice. To keep your users engaged, you need to organise your content.

Chapter Seven: Sell Online Coaching

Online coaching is similar to selling your courses online. The only difference is that coaching is more direct and hands-on because you need to be directly involved in education. Again, coaching is not limited to academic fields. You can provide coaching on fitness, crafts, or even online gaming. Here is how you can turn online coaching into a source of income.

Build an Audience

The first step is to find and create a customer base. There are many ways to approach this:

Website

Starting your own website and build your credibility by posting an article every week to display your experience in the field. For instance, if you are a fitness coach, then you can write about some of the food that fitness enthusiasts must avoid. Of course, try to make the article title catchy, the content short, sweet, and with plenty of keywords so that your content is easily discovered.

Email

You can incorporate email subscription into your blog posts so that you can deliver more contents directly to your audience's (and possibly potential customer) mailbox.

Social Media

Social media platforms such as Facebook allow you to create your own group to have all of your audience in one place in addition to allowing them to ask questions or create their own posts easier.

Go Live

Facebook allows you to interact directly with your audience, which boosts your credibility.

Expand

Utilise other social media platforms such as Instagram or Pinterest that lead viewers straight to your website and articles.

With your marketing net cast wide and people starting to visit and interact with you, it is time to give them more value.

Launch Premium Offer

There are two ways you can approach service offering - One-off coaching or subscription-based coaching services. When it comes to how you can offer such a service, it really depends on you. For example, if you offer fitness coaching services, then you can provide your customers with videos with certain exercises for the whole week as well as worksheets to help them arrange their diets. You can also offer them other materials to help them in their endeavour.

Set Up Your Launch

A good way to set things off is by launching a webinar, which is a seminar hosted on the web. It is a good idea that you present at least three times at different times of the day to account for different time zones and schedules of your potential customers.

Email List

To get the words out there, you can send emails directly to your subscribers as well as those who are in your Facebook Group, Instagram followers, etc. A good way to approach this is to provide everyone with a 3-part email sequence for those in your email list, starting with you informing them about the webinar, the time, and content you will discuss, and then lead them up to the registration link if they are interested.

Update Your Pages

Remember all of those articles you have written in the past to generate traffic and build credibility? Edit all of them and add a handy section at the end to let your audience know about the upcoming webinar as well as a form to let them sign up.

Post on Social Media Outlets

Make sure that your followers on Facebook, Instagram, Twitter, etc. know about your webinar and funnel them to your registration page.

Ads

You can even create Facebook Ads to get the words out there even more.

Launch

When the day of the webinar arrives, there are a few things you need to know. First of all, make sure you address the one thing that your audience is desperate to find. For instance, if it is a fitness webinar, then let them know about all the celebrities manage to stay fit even in their elderly age. If it is a gaming webinar, then let them know about how all the top players in the game manage to be effective in each match.

The idea behind getting so many people to join is that you never know which one of them will actually sign up for your services. With so many people attending, even if only 1% of the attendees sign up, you will have plenty of customers to get you a sizeable income.

After that, it is just a matter of repeating the whole process every three months or so to get more people on board.

Chapter Eight: Dropshipping Store

Dropshipping is similar to owning a shop, but you do not need to have a stock of products at hand. All orders for any products you received will be forwarded to the manufacturer or wholesale retailer, who will ship the product to the customer directly. Therefore, you do not handle or even see the product. Here's how you do it.

Pick the Right Product

If done correctly, dropshipping is one of the easiest and quickest way to generate a steady stream of passive income. However, many people stumble when it comes to laying the foundation, which is crucial for the success of such a business. The initial time investment is also required. Knowing what product to sell to what group of people are critical.

Create a Professional Website

The next step is to find a place to host your product. Thankfully, you do not need to sink in a huge amount of time to build a flashy, professional website anymore. Many website builders out there make it a breeze to create your very own website at a very low cost. If you do not want to have a personal website, then social media is a good place to start because it serves as a place to advertise your business anyway.

Find the Right Supplier

Your supplier is responsible for supplying the product as well as delivering it straight to your customers. Therefore, you need someone who is reliable.

Be Consistent

In order to generate a steady flow of passive income from dropshipping, you need to invest a good amount of time on growing your customer base. This can be done through consistent and quality services as well as active marketing either on your blog post, social media, or personal website.

Conclusion

With all the basics in your grasp, the next step is to get out there and start planning and taking action. Making a lot of money from passive income is not easy at the start because you need to invest a lot of time into the project at the start while making little to no money at all. This has discouraged many people. If you have a great idea but have doubts, remember that everyone else who follows the same path also had the same doubts. However, they kept their heads down and followed through with their plans, and succeeded. You will most likely find success if you do the same.

At the very least, it is better to acknowledge that you are wrong and learn from your mistakes rather than regret not exploring other options while you still can. It is also worth mentioning that, just like anything else in life, you will fail quite a few times trying to get the ball rolling.

Another thing worth mentioning is that you should start with your very own website or social media page because you can easily establish many other sources of passive income. If you have a YouTube channel with many subscribers, you can easily advertise your other products and services.

With that in mind, I wish you the best of luck.